4/15

FLOODS

BY PETER MURRAY

The Child's World

Published by The Child's World®
1980 Lookout Drive • Mankato, MN 56003-1705
800-599-READ • www.childsworld.com

ACKNOWLEDGMENTS
The Child's World®: Mary Berendes, Publishing Director
Olivia Gregory Editing

PHOTO CREDITS
© Bjmcse/Dreamstime.com: 18; Johan Larson/Shutterstock.com:
21; jpegisclair/BigStock.com: 13; MAHATHIR MOHD YASIN/
Shutterstock.com: 5; Maria Luisa Lopez Estivill/Dreamstime.
com: cover, 1; Melissa Brandes/Shutterstock.com: 10; Patryk
Kosmider/Shutterstock.com: 15; Pavel L Photo and Video/
Shutterstock.com: 7; Umkehrer/Shutterstock.com: 9

ISBN 9781631437656
LCCN 2014945417

Printed in the United States of America
Mankato, MN
November, 2014
PA02245

ABOUT THE AUTHOR

Peter Murray has written more than 80 children's books on science, nature, history, and other topics. He also writes novels for adults and teens under the name Pete Hautman. An animal lover, Peter lives in Golden Valley, Minnesota, in a house with one woman, two poodles, several dozen spiders, thousands of microscopic dust mites, and an occasional mouse.

Table of Contents

All Life Needs Water

Everybody needs water. We need water to drink. We bathe in it. We cook with it. We swim in it. We water our gardens, we wash our clothes, we fill squirt guns and water balloons.

Our bodies are made mostly of water. Without water we would crumble into dust. But what happens when there is too much water?

It's very important to drink lots of fresh water.

Spring Rains

Every spring it rains. The water soaks into the earth. The water that the soil cannot hold runs into the streams and gullies. The extra water flows into lakes and rivers. Every spring, the rivers rise. The water is held back by the banks, or sometimes it spreads into the surrounding wetlands. When the rain stops, the water level slowly drops. But what happens when the rain keeps on falling?

In the spring of 1993, people all across the Midwestern United States wondered when the rain would stop. It rained in April. It rained in May. It rained in June and in July. In Iowa, some places got three feet (1 m) of rain during those months—a whole year's worth of rain in just four months!

The rivers and lakes were full, and the ground was soaked. There was no place for the water to go. It kept on raining. Every few days, there would be another downpour. Every week, the rivers rose higher.

Spring rains come with cloudy, sometimes gloomy, weather. It's always a good idea to have an umbrella and boots handy in the spring!

Too Much Rain

Just two feet (0.6 m) of water has enough force to carry away a car.

River flooding is the most common type of flooding.

When there is too much rain, rivers rise above their banks and flood the surrounding land. The low-lying land on each side of a river is called a **floodplain**. When settlers first came to America, they discovered that the soil in the floodplains was good for growing crops. Unfortunately, every few years the land would flood, and their crops would be washed away. Earthen banks called **levees** and walls called **dikes** were built to keep the rivers from flooding the land. The dikes and levees made the floodplains safe. Or so people thought!

Nobody knew how much rain would fall in 1993. In June and July, rivers in the Midwest rose as much as 50 feet (15 m). Thousands of soldiers and volunteers spent day after day piling up sandbags to reinforce the levees. But the rain kept on falling. Billions of gallons of water spilled over the banks and levees, flooding farms and cities in nine states.

This person is stacking bags of sand to keep the floodwaters away.

The city of Des Moines, Iowa was waist-deep in water. People swam through their houses trying to save a few possessions. Farmers watched their fields turn into lakes. They had to rescue their pigs and chickens in rowboats. And it kept on raining!

They called it the "Great Flood of 1993." More than 20 million acres (more than 8 million hectares) were flooded. Fifty people died.

By the autumn of 1993, most of the flooded land had dried out. Houses and businesses were rebuilt. Fields were replanted. Dikes and levees were repaired. But some of the floodplain was left in its natural state. The 1993 flood was especially bad because the water had no place to go. The next time the rivers rise, the floodplain will help absorb the extra water.

The Great Flood of 1993 caused $15 billion worth of damage.

A very dangerous time can come after a flood is over. When waters go down, areas that were flooded can become contaminated by debris, fuel, and even sewage.

The Great Flood of 1993 caused roads, yards, and farmland to be completely underwater.

Hurricanes

People who live near the ocean sometimes get soaked by a different type of flood. **Hurricanes** are gigantic, powerful storms that form far out at sea. A big hurricane can dump billions of tons of rain in minutes. Its winds can reach speeds of 200 miles (322 km) per hour, causing enormous waves.

When a hurricane approaches land, it pushes a huge mound of water in front of it. This gigantic wave, called a **storm surge**, can be 20 feet (6 m) high. Between the rain and the storm surge, things get wet fast! Buildings, trees, people, and animals can be swept away in the rushing water.

Flooding from hurricanes has caused some of the worst disasters in history. On August 29, 2005, Hurricane Katrina struck the Gulf Coast. Almost all of New Orleans flooded, and the water didn't go down for weeks! More than 1,800 people died in this disaster.

These people could only get around by canoe after Hurricane Katrina flooded their New Orleans neighborhood in 2005.

Tsunamis

Most floods are caused by too much rain. But some floods are caused by undersea earthquakes or volcanoes. When the bottom of the ocean suddenly moves, the water above it must also move. This creates a long, low wave called a **tsunami**. The tsunami moves across the ocean at speeds of up to 500 miles (805 km) per hour. As the wave reaches the shallow water near shore, it rises up to tremendous heights—sometimes over 100 feet (30 m)! A tsunami can occur without warning.

On December 26, 2004, a deadly tsunami hit the coasts of 11 countries along the Indian Ocean. Waves were over 50 feet high (15 m) at times. More than 150,000 people died, and millions of people were left homeless.

This memorial park in Thailand is full of boats and ships that were pushed over a half mile (1 km) ashore in the 2004 tsunami.

Floods from Dams

The Johnstown Flood happened on May 31, 1889.

The Johnstown Flood is sometimes called the "Great Flood of 1889."

The Johnstown Flood was the first major disaster-relief effort handled by the American Red Cross.

Sometimes floods are caused by people. In 1852, engineers built a huge dam of rocks and mud across the Little Conemaugh River in Pennsylvania. This South Fork Dam was 931 feet (284 m) long and 72 feet (22 m) high. Where the river was plugged by the dam, the water got deep and created Lake Conemaugh. The lake was two miles (3 km) long and 70 feet (21 m) deep. People used this new lake for fishing and boating. A few miles downstream, thousands of people lived in a city called Johnstown. Sometimes they joked about what would happen if the dam broke. But nobody thought it would really happen.

The South Fork Dam held for almost 40 years. But on Memorial Day in 1889, a record rainfall caused the dam to burst. A wall of water 50 feet (15 m) high rushed down the valley at 40 miles (64 km) per hour. The people of Johnstown had no warning.

The water hit the city like a monstrous, wet bulldozer, ripping up houses and trees and shattering brick buildings. A railroad train was washed off its tracks. Some people escaped by floating away on the roofs of their houses. But 2,209 people died.

Here you can see the damage after the Johnstown Flood of 1889.

Most floods happen by accident. They arc caused by unexpected rain, storms, earthquakes, or by a dam-builder's mistake. But the deadliest flood in modern history was caused on purpose.

In 1938, China was being invaded by Japan. The Japanese were winning. The Chinese forces were desperate. To stop the Japanese, Chinese soldiers blew up dikes on the Huang He River. They stopped the Japanese advance, but victory came at a terrible cost. One million Chinese people died in that flood.

The Huang He River is also called the Yellow River. The deadliest floods in history havo all been along this river.

The Yellow River is the third-longest river in Asia. It is the sixth-longest river in the world.

Here is how the Yellow River in Ningxia, China looks from the sky.

The Risk of Floods

If you come into contact with flood water, be sure to wash the area with clean water and soap—flood water is very dirty and can make you sick.

Sometimes people are willing to risk floods because the land is good to them in other ways. People live near rivers because the farmland is fertile and because the rivers are important for transportation. They say, "Next time, the levees will hold!" People live along coasts because they like to be close to the ocean. They say, "A hurricane will never strike here!" People live downstream from huge dams because they trust the engineers who built them. They say, "That dam will never break!"

And they hope they are right!

This playground is underwater after heavy rain and flooding in Queensland, Australia.